DESIRE PATH

desire
path

poems

TARYN HUBBARD

TALONBOOKS

Talonbooks
9259 Shaughnessy Street, Vancouver, British Columbia, Canada V6P 6R4
talonbooks.com

Talonbooks is located on xʷməθkʷəy̓əm, Sḵwx̱wú7mesh, and səl̓ilwətaʔɬ Lands.

First printing: 2020

Typeset in Minion
Printed and bound in Canada on 100% post-consumer recycled paper

Interior and cover design and illustration by andrea bennett

Talonbooks acknowledges the financial support of the Canada Council for the Arts, the Government of Canada through the Canada Book Fund, and the Province of British Columbia through the British Columbia Arts Council and the Book Publishing Tax Credit.

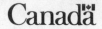

LIBRARY AND ARCHIVES CANADA CATALOGUING IN PUBLICATION

Title: Desire path / Taryn Hubbard.
Names: Hubbard, Taryn, author.
Description: Poems.
Identifiers: Canadiana 20200179454 | ISBN 9781772012637 (SOFTCOVER)
Classification: LCC PS8615.U2183 D47 2020 | DDC C811/.6—dc23

For my family

Desires are already memories.

—Italo Calvino, *Invisible Cities* (1972)

Contents

DESIRE PATH

HEIRLOOM

1.

I was born across from the first
McDonald's in Canada,

outside of Vancouver,
where the airport is, greenhouses,

long straight roads we drive
so fast.

My first words were upsized, waxy,
drowned

in a syrup that stayed with me,
soaking

into everything I tried to say
until I lost that desire

between the muffled sounds
of the drive-thru speaker,

and I kept my words there, broken,
gently purring, repeating

orders back toward
idling cars. Some nights

my head lay closest
to the window in silence until

a dump truck,
a motorcycle, the flash of light

exposing everything barely keeping
this place standing.

2.

One year goes by
then another, another

until my time is stacked
high around, and I look

to see I've formed a line,
a threat, a jack-

knifed semi-trailer blocking
rush hour, a continuous

descent from something beyond me.
Still-sweet liquid IV,

though one thing I'll reframe,
from the start, is

the fact I'm working
doesn't mean I'm bored.

The fact I'm making plans,
cutting corners,

severing feet, swimming for
retweets, cracking dreams, striving

toward an unknown future
means only I'm trying.

I am trying
and that's my worry.

3.

If I pull the text close enough to my eyes

I can understand the words as written

but not the intention behind them or the history

or the eyes that read these words in the free community newspaper

and thought: *That's where we'll go now.*

The words are cut from an ad for a house marketed as "Grandma's Country Charmer."

The faded paper shows this:

a small black and white photo of a very old house.

Perhaps it was a converted barn, it never felt solid and the foundation was mud.

It had a horse carriage in the backyard. We burned it down one night after dinner.

The flames felt nice because it was always cold and damp.

Even the moon was divided.

4.

From Richmond and the long roads, we went to Surrey down the highway where we lived in Grandma's Country Charmer, a hundred-year-old bungalow next to a small, independent drive-thru that applied a similar clown theme as McDonald's applied to selling fast-food burgers in hopes of a similar multinational success. I bet the owners wanted to be billionaires, and figured success was as easy as copying those who were already successful. So they had a clown that was red and yellow, too, because that's what made McDonald's McDonald's and them the Next Big Thing.

Decades later, I worked with someone who wore red and yellow weekly and called it their ketchup-and-mustard outfit. The work I did involved looking into other people's calendars to find opportunities to take more of their time, to wedge one appointment against another until there was nothing left to occupy and my time was spent. This work lasted longer than the restaurant beside our family house.

When the restaurant was torn down, the rats came, or maybe they were already there to begin with, and had been so for many years, happily eating what they could find in the kitchen. When they came to our house, the rats were already as long as footballs, like genetically modified spaghetti squashes with eyes, and I'd watch them dive into the holes in our floors as if it were nothing, as if it were a sincere form of domestic caring.

5.

The path forward begins with a reference to what was left behind.
Or something.

WAYFINDING

The suburban highway
links signs
            attention pinches
stuck
logos cast in plastic

it's hard to find
the idea of here
and there
from a form
that grew only
with the idea of
car & home

meet me at the Chevron
meet me at the 7-Eleven
meet me where the median
divides this road
with
            crosswalk in dash cams
            eight-lane spans –

next year the city
will be longer

            stretch and
stretched further
into the woods

            darkness
brightened
with high beams

SUNRISE

Run past methadone
clinic strip. Clients
curbside gum ash-soggy
Zig-Zag pack spit.

Where ya going so fast?
ya gonna make it?

Over five-hundred acres of
here and available. Parking
lot crust piss-rust
car shells yellow signs "Brake Jobs
in 1 Hour."

In this city, everything is so
far apart. That's the issue.

Guy with raccoon-tail
keychain stands by
window "All Men Must
Be Accompanied by Wife."

Sorry, We're Open.

A stove, 1972 model.
Top Quality.
$200 OBO.

YES, WE PAWN SHOP

How will I rein this in?

A view corridor, not really. But a long distance of Grouse Mountain still.

Cheap land / great potential / close to transit / a cook's kitchen.

"Remember your reusable bags."

Avoid City Parkway.

Surrey girls give great head.

Home of North America's only triple-X triplex.

My friend played Whalley Little League. His dad coached

and fixed cars in the Superstore parking lot.

If you have concepts, please enter contest to stop sprawl. Gift cards!

It takes money to change the names of streets.

I pledge to put an end to sprawl. It is unsightly, and we deserve better.

How could he be building a grow op back there? He said hi to me?

Yaletown used to be a rail yard. Believe it.

You know the one about Surrey girls?

INVERTED TRIANGLE

For Sale
       Land for High-rise
(cell #)
potential
R-SF to CD-multi
       motivated
rezoned
asphalt
faded, crumbling crack
shack removed
       squatters pop-up
tent
community
reputation what
are you?
       (XXX)
I keep
forget. Remember the first
service station:
sold ice,
water, gas,
air. Rented cabins
       round back. No
hope for train
station in this town. Land
dirt, trees, wild
animal noises,
lots. Spaces for
parking.

CURBSIDE

A little market sells single cigs –

The Byrd Exotic Showroom is done up Viva Vegas –

The Blue Corvette Lounge

Before it shut

Hung its cobalt sign

Over the highway

Studded with sparkle

Shone like shredded

Pop cans whenever the wind

Wanted

MOVE

Jumbo letterings
activate sky
and headspace.

This space is now available!

Look all the way up
the side of the glass
building in construction
and the sun reflected
washes my whole sight
over. Vicious.

The people that preside
on this real-estate billboard?
They laugh because they're
joyous, blessed, kissed
jaundiced as if yellow
fell from rose-
hips of a limitless future.

What drives YOU?

I'm not sure. This pressure
is not easy. Direct messaging
yanks the aspiration down
to my level, but I never wanted it.

It's not that I lack drive
or imagination,
it's that I feel there's a black hole
smack in the objective.

I feel it with the *no guarantee*
asterisks wavering above this longing
at the scale of a watermelon.

Home is a stretch goal
sold out, stickered over,
and when rain hits us
sideways, water slips
from this billboard
onto the heads of passing
commuters.

Our heads.

WATCH

Action on this TV is big enough to see from the street. My neighbours watch TV because shows on streaming services are very good now. Most people who drive this street can tell this is just a shack with a huge TV and a naked single-pane window. The neighbour quoted in the *Province* after the police incident that blocked the road all day with yellow tape did not know. Most shows are like movies now. It's all star power and true-crime scripts, protagonists duking it out with rivals. Hairspray and cheekbones. The bungalow houses from the 1960s have these big windows looking in on their raised front rooms, it's a defining feature. The bungalows on this street will not be remodeled like on HGTV. "Troublesome properties," and the landlord is assumed absentee. Entire streets summed up: suburbs are bad for health.

PAVE WAY

Until thens left over
swallow heaps of asphalt.
Lick, taste tar.

What a hassle. Meds
make me feel to be. No
thens, little nevers.

It's just how much juice
to keep a street's
whisper. A shell from the ocean

sounds like what we think
it sounds like. One day we
will say *That looks so over*.

And wonder what of us really stays
before tiny heart flees. Sick
for waiting.

SUBURB LAND STRIP

Raise a concern.

Tell the pawnshop guy
in Starbucks I've got to see a girl
over a missed economic
boom.

Roll up the rim
on Best Buy / Loblaws
speckled
super blocks.

We now offer
state-of-the-argh,
where are the parents?

I took from someone
and now feel stasis.

Can't talk now,
but the city between goal posts
is a culmination
of various bad habits,
frequent misunderstandings.

Should I believe
what you said
about the future
of this place or not?

For a social anxiety silver bullet –
try the bedroom community
after dark.

When I can't sleep for days,
I lament the deep dreams
I won't have the chance to forget.

BROKEN TRIANGLE

Fold old parking lot
in and in
drive awkward
three-point intersection.

This triangle-shaped plot outs
parking stall pushing,
anti-urban
invites you to come, sit.

We'll do it better (then)
drive up and (then)
drive thru (then) about
time to gas up.

Fold triangle half over. Still
hide three points
wish concrete edges dry
pressure rainbow potholes for

this space takes on more
cigarette butts, advance
lefts. Thin grass seed
kicks up.

V3T

after Sachiko Murakami

Here condos named Quattro Ethical
Gardens Access Evo Park Place The Brookland.

Thinly (sub)urban no place every
nowhere. Surrey City Centre, Whalley. This.

Here by-the-hour stays Econo Lodge Flamingo
Motor Hotel Surrey City Centre Motel Super 8.

I'm sorry about the mess. Pressure wash
the streets. They come back dirty.

Here a good place to (re)move from. Buy
next to SkyTrain / freeway / bus loop.

Here billboard covers pothole lots. Projects
watercolour high-rise, a paycheque, reasonable strata fees.

Here a strip of shops South Indian Jamaican East
Indian Vietnamese Ukrainian Korean Pawn.

Here a neighbourhood (re)named City Centre. Headquarters
in the old Whalley mall. Updated designer paint.

MARKERS

At the time of writing: gas is $1.71 a litre in the commuter neighbour-hoods along Highway 1 heading into Vancouver. The streets are empty, the houses are far apart including the empty lots saved for a rainy day when it will be more advantageous to redevelop them into something with suburban density, which is code for a strip of three-story town-houses cut apart like pieces of bread.

Why do interior designers decorate townhouse presentation centres to look like microbrewery tasting rooms? How many growlers and acoustic guitars and inspirational-quote posters does a couple of carefree young professionals need?

I like the part of books where a writer takes note of the cost of certain staples. Sometimes that's the main observation grounding the work to its time.

At the time of writing: bread hovers around $2.50 for the regular GMO stuff. I am not an authority on buying organic or hyper-local or gluten-free, though I'd know where to get it. Bread prices have gone down in major grocery chains across the country after it was discovered they were intentionally overpricing for years.

The year before writing: bread was $3.79. If you read some CanLit that put bread around three or so bucks, it wasn't true.

We know more now but shop at the same stores.

Suspend discussion of the present by pointing to the aspirational.

Nice kid.

FIND A WAY HOME

Nightclub draws
crowds,

police cruiser. CHEAP
BUD TUES

leaves floors slick. The
puddles outside pool

spit – it'll be okay, let it wash
away with the forecasted

rain. All these people
drove here but come

morning not a car'll be
in sight.

SOUNDS ONLY YOUTH CAN HEAR

On steps where one
might sleep public
alarms chime reminders
to go.

What a difference
an alarm makes at
decibels only youth
should hear.

A reckless buzz
every endless day
scatters people
across the highway, even.

I can hear the alarm
above the traffic
in front of the methadone clinic
across four lanes.

Its high pitch chirps, *away away,*
away away.

MOON SCHEDULE

Cement stairs left
over. Four thick slabs

moss-slick welcome
unwelcome visitors to lot.

A home removed. Remainder
gypsum board chunk, heavy

rain-plunged T-shirts. Do
you remember this house?

Phantom shingles. My boot
stuck in mud. Mostly

puddle and cigarette butts.
Hookups left open. That

frustrating glassless house flew
orange tarp sails before demo. This

spot where I'd walk up
to your room. Tonight's super

moon smooths what
foundation's left

to sidewalk's cut edge
this property's all dug

up, rimmed with stomped
Lucky Lager, surrendered

deposit.

REPEAT (I)

If you dumpster
dive. Find perogies.
Buck
cabbage rolls.
Disposed.
Left only to turn you
on.

Wonder it lonesome.
Beside a liquor
store with
Baron's beer
cheaper per oz. than
Molson Canadian.

Behind the Hertz
car rental,
I can't think
of hanging anywhere
else.

IN THE AFTERNOON

Outside
the train station
steps hold commuters
coming going.
        A plaza
spray-painted white,
"DON'T TOUCH."

For forty bucks get an unlocked iPhone
thirty a T-shirt with silver flourish
fifteen adobo, rice, 2L Coke
toonie pizza slice
thirty thousand a unit
reserved / no GST promo.

The bus loop dons title of
city centre
a schedule of routes tied
briefly before unraveling
down major arterials.

Moments
between sidewalks
and almost-empty lots except
        the one plastic
lawn chair on nest egg
easement, an option to turn grass
into wider driving.

Commuter hearts
start like the engines of diesel
trucks when field across
station, free for all-day parking,
gets dug up.

Update
        "NEW PAY PARKING"
stalls for rent
between line drawn.

Touch rough-cut iridescence
left from a windshield
thrown down.

        the bus is empty (or)
        there is too much of a line (or)
        I saw a fist fight at my stop one time for no reason!

Jump fences
        of the afternoon, jump
triangle stacks of failed asphalt kick
a rain-soaked curb couch.

        It's not a real mayflower.

It's a Slurpee cup soaked through.

INVENTORY BUSH

This morning landscapers shaved the south side of the cedars so we
could see in and nothing could hide again, and shopping bags candy
wrappers beer cans water bottles cigarette butts cigarette wrappers Tim
Hortons cups socks papers posters for lost cats condoms gum bottle
caps burger wrappers lighters crayon drawings by little kids glass shards
liquidation flyers cheap rubbish removal ads strands of hair coffee-cup
lids and razors flee from phantom underbrush onto sidewalk, and this
debris will be swept away and the cuts on the limbs could be counted
and maybe they have rings too to mark the years these bushes served as
a community's container, but what's left are skinny sticks that jut.

MALL ACCESS

The mall doesn't board
vacant retail space, just papers.

Empty store windows soften with stock
images of shopping-bag women.

FIRE SALE. LIQUIDATION.
CHEAP FIXTURES. 10% OFF.

On the bottom floor an exit removed
by the barber/Autoplan,

the Boston Pizza, just up from the spinning
hotdogs at the juice stand. Dead

hallways with yellow tape draped like pageantry. Do not
cross.

Upstairs Keno, tiny tables full of scratch-
and-win flick left over from a winner, maybe.

WEIGHTED KEYS

Electric piano mumble takes
drive-thru window tone
and throws it across balconies.

Notes over lawnmowers
semi truck long brake
score for the kid playing basketball.

The times I see the people in my building
we think it's on fire.
Pray alarm sprinklers don't

wash away home.
On the curb waiting for the firefighters' *All
clear don't know good to go*

a girl jogs by. Maybe
she's headed for the Olympics
and maybe the electric keyboardist

who lives in building A
will practice all night long.

COMMUNICATION

Three pharmacies on strip blinking lights red on storefront bars boys swing awning boots on window West Whalley Ring Road renamed University Drive on plan "You Are Under Surveillance" on sign *Here's a can of Old Milwaukee* stop tapping on driver's side highly unlikely the house can be restored on listing all trespassers will be executed [*sic*] on blue fence I got stainless granite laminate for less than rent! on back-page ad a rebrand a re-establish a readjust.

DEAR 203B

I take my boots off
at elevator
when troubled

cat gallops through
rooms are for sleeping
on a bed with wheels

outside that one night
we swore pop was gun-
shot but action

movies rise through
your ceiling, neighbour, the
end of the universe

pulses in a setting far away
but familiar if we were better
looking outside trees

crowd our window glass
tower reflects
Subway, Moneytree, ocean

of asphalt cracked
a million directions parking
is free in the new "190 Stall

Lot" forever, well, not forever ever,
but that's fine, I prefer to stay in and
listen to you.

REPEAT (II)

If you notice
after house crisp
all drive creep
hope
charcoal hawks less.

What's your per-square-foot
selling price, considering?

It's a fact, remained
since plan version 3
rev. 2: a property teardown
is worth as much as a
tax assessment.

NIGHT CLASS

Drudge street
dry wring
loose skirt
hem to finger-
tips affix fists, ready.

Flatten tatter
city fragments
turn off ear-
buds, listen soft
hey-you.

Zip up, step up
shoulders back toward
tough enough
side-swipe
shadow creep.

Call your friend
call your mom
call your wonder
listen to the tone
ask gently, *How are you tonight?*

Jaywalk sprint, cross
empty lot look back once
then eyes
forward. When the Buick
slows, run.

In tonight's class you read
of women in distress –
loves, flames.

On the radio, you learn
anything can be used
as a weapon
for self-defence
even your house
key.

CAN'T FORCE A GHOST

Warm ghosts are the best ghosts to invite over, I invite them, and together we conjure ambition in a ten-foot-high barrier along the south side of a clay yard. My yard. A family spot where the dog can escape the other three sides. It's not a proper fence. It's a wall. No matter. The thing is: the wall is where we weigh days, where gray bricks shadow our lives. A barrier to keep out disruptions. The distractions come anyway. When my neighbour is a suburban neighbourhood pub. When Maggie goes running down the street after drinking four Long Island iced teas, no dinner. Wonder about Long Island and running and the voice that shouts through the ghosts milling on the sidewalk, *Maggie, I'm so sorry. Just come back, baby. Come back, bay-be. Shit.*

INTROVERT'S SOCIAL HANGOVER

Indeed. It's the yelling. A professional suicide tugging at my heart sleeve that needs to talk directly to you. In the preface we were warned the text could start shouting back at us at any moment. And out leapt letters dressed in sans serif boas. This is to say the best we can do is the worst we can make up. I came here, originally, to toss spent lottery tickets in the glass bottles thoughtfully separated from the weekly recycling. We are so close to speaking in synthetic tongues that one day it may be more effective to bleed these words as they leave my lips than project them.

SHADELESS

I was active in my attending.

Sentenced to painting lumpy plaster on my bedroom wall.

A mother's loneliness passed down through dishrags and hair combs.

I drove all the way around.

The house waited across from the five-pin bowling alley.

The family sat inside their container

and listened to the softness of gutter-ball-tossing speedway gamblers.

I drove all the way around to find something closer.

The hundred-watt bulb on the bedroom ceiling shone without cover.

Still, it was light, which I needed.

The light was bright, but I kept my eyes on it.

If I looked directly up, then over, I could see auras on the plaster,

the inner auras of these rotting walls.

I could see the walls were violet, and I settled into a feeling of violet.

Violet, violet for many days.

IMPOSSIBLE SUPERSTITION

A knife in the door jam.

A house locked shut.

I had to wipe my eyes twice
when I saw it.

For safety reasons, the dolphins bob
in my brain and not beside the boat.

The sounds from the street are in my toes
not in my ears.

And in late August the spiders come in to cozy
up to us.

They want to find a peaceful place to rest
and we let them.

Mom in the nursery planting flowers from seed
dad cuts mirror.

When the mirror shatters, it's
swept together.

When a mirror breaks each day
the bad luck penetrates more lifetimes

than we could ever count, but still I count
them. I count them down.

WIN

In the morning I wake
and think casinos. It's the
promise of luck that
sandblasts the sighs
straight from our guts,
the idea of easy.

We thought our life
built beside a casino
was all we could ask for,
its 24-hour automation

bringing us through
a conveyor of joy.
Those coos from the slot
machines crawled

in our ears,
laying shiny, slithering
eggs. We could
hear the call forth from

anywhere. Those days
the bananas went
straight from green to
spotted, and

I wouldn't tell the doctor this –
I wouldn't tell a doctor anything.

FLAGPOLE

One summer I walk the same path each day with the idea of creating a
folded corner on a very specific patch of grass

I try to cut the boulevard's angle that holds the part of King George
Boulevard and 104 Avenue that leads commuters on and off the Pattullo
Bridge and into New Westminster then Burnaby then Vancouver for
the work day

There's a checkered racing flag here waving in the wind above chain-link
with Comic Sans lettering, "USED CARS"

I chose this exact grass because it's part of my day and I'm aware of my
feet and how they move to trace my invisible steps from the walk before
with nothing to guide me except the street, the curb, the time of day, the
shoes on my feet, even the garbage that wind's displayed in the chain-
link for drivers in gridlock to notice

I walk this path twenty times a month, twice per day, more on the week-
ends and the grass sticks back up

FORECASTS

You were the strange kid.
A little voice knows it.

If you call your neighbour now,
he will drag you down
to his level and beat you.

The news spreads
in two-hundred word posts.
Pray no one notices.

What do they see in you, anyway?

Important milestones you eventually learn
you must plan for:
    unhindered growth, unending joy,
unmotivated friendship.

Success is understanding the essence of *un*,
and believing in it.

What will you give in exchange
for a wide range of knowing?

If you are lucky,
investing will repay you many times.

If you are fortunate,
investing will confess
your secrets free of surcharge
or special handling.

Take a risk but do not rush:
patience is preparation in moonlight.

MILKY-PINK WINDOW GLASS

at night time, a near-death feeling of paralysis
            a small edge
of my brain awakes

a shovel of rocks, no, a fist
full, fly against
the single-pane window

how many times must we get up to chase him away?

that evening was for playing ghost games, a way not to scare ourselves,
but ask truths of those who've left us

we ask them if there's anything we should know

nah

or did we mishear? We want there to be something

gravel on the window

he'd called us that day to warn us of his visit, if only we'd understood the
meaning behind his sick slobbering on the telephone receiver or his

desire to subvert our sleep

BOARDED-UP STRIP MALL CHURCH

The church beside the One-Hour Dry Cleaning where I did Brownies.
When I first listened to Kurt Cobain. When I said my first "fuck" in
front of my dad, who said, *"Don't say that so loud"* but not *"Don't say
that."* Where years later my friends and I would try to find a way to
sneak through the fence to see what was left inside so we could reprise
our chant one last time: *"We're here to lend a hand / To love our God
/ And serve our Queen ..."* But never did. Too risky. Kept walking. The
boarded-up strip mall church that eventually burned down. Said to have
been by hands of mischief. Boredom. The plot where a new mall went
up so fast. One with a Subway. Where we'd sit on the back steps and
throw our pickles at the glass door as it swung closed like ceremony.

BIRTHDAY

You have dressed
as a clown this day.

Your pants are homemade
from bright flags

once hung by the town
Business Improvement Association.

We're pleased to have reclaimed this fabric
from the ultimate dumpster in the sky.

We covered the opossum on the sidewalk
playing possum with an apple box.

This may well have been the birthday
game.

Apparent death is soft, seductive.
But it can't change you.

I thought you'd planted these beautiful
flowers for me

that if I swallowed a lemon seed
a tree would take root in my stomach and that'd be it.

To burst with citrus is to become
much stranger than before.

Our fish pond filled with cow
manure leaves nowhere for the goldfish to go.

All morning we played games
I'd never win in a million years.

MATTER

I try identifying the opportunist versus the bully, the bully versus the
one who sees an opportunity in everyone they meet. I take the makeup
off my cheeks and gently add it to the pile headed to the biofuel plant.
A frozen brain is one sign the shadows are doing what they're supposed
to. The look of the day was to downplay one's more austere features
with expensive bubble-gum fill. I didn't think of walking as a way of
understanding until I broke a bank of small rocks over my ankles. The
direction forward is full-fat yogurt and EV parking. The night he yelled
graveyard from the bath I summoned a personal truth about working
non-standard hours. One week it was three pounds of apples and the
next it was five, and each one of them I ate off a blade. I watched two
happy woodpeckers become increasingly disturbed by my presence and
thought, *of course they would*. Of course the application for the bank
was lost under a flat of sugar-free pop. As a material collector, I put
everything into my bag, even the coupon for a tire rotation for a 4 × 4
I do not own. Slowly, I learned to cuddle my rage with thoughtfully
applied pressure. Psychologically, it was better to scroll the news than
seek it out. Still, it could be worse. Still, I could remember to turn the
front light on when it's dark enough.

LITTLE HOLUBTSI

A storm of matryoshka dolls
spills from between my hips
and onto the floor.

We hadn't noticed
they'd been waiting there
populating.

It was a surprise, even
for me, though
we didn't speak of it.

And now they're dancing
on your gleaming green linoleum
because you're dancing, too.

What does this say about
how close I pay attention
to what I'm doing?

On afternoons spent peeling
back layers of boiled cabbage
my fingers go numb.

This is probably because
I think things will be easier
than they are.

When the dolls re-nest,
we miss them – the way
they didn't talk, just moved.

How attached we'd become
to something we didn't know
we wanted.

Gain something unexpected
and it's with you. It's all
so necessary so quickly.

ATTEMPTS

When you have a treasure, *accept it right from the start.*

So I do. I start over. Start over and over again, like I should have from the beginning.

I *have* a treasure, and it's starting to manifest.

The treasure was a state that took hold late July when the air was hot and thick with smoke from wildfires three hours east of us in the Interior. The ash felt like living and I felt like living ash. I hadn't expected this manifestation and was absent from what was happening in my body; I went about my day.

I knew myself (or believed as much) but still, everything that grew in me came as a surprise. Still, it was growing.

The afternoon was like any other, but the smoke.

The smoke stung my nose and eyes and mouth and sunk between the fissures of my brain in order to connect with every aspect of me, and there was nothing I could do, and I went about my business as if there was nothing wrong with what I was breathing and what I was tasting and what I was seeing and what I was thinking.

The smoke was from the wildfires hours away. I inhaled these fires as I walked to and from the bus to work. I read about their origin online.

I took the air in like it was, a necessity.

Slowly, among all this smoke, I felt the inside of me growing tender.

Downward
drift.

Come again, a cycle.

Drift and drift and drift. Come dirty,
dirty drift. Come

again, and

again.

Wires got crossed.

The days seemed to shorten, and the wind kept coming toward us from out east where hundreds of fires sucked up all the trees and houses and barns in their path.

I was on autopilot. I thought I knew what I sensed. I was willing to try, to start over: gather up everything and attempt again. Try, try.

Still, my belly began to grow only I didn't know it, didn't understand the connection to what I was experiencing.

The air was hazy and stalked me. It was dirty and dangerous and immersed my body.

I read the social media about the attempts to halt the fires. I read the comments posted by avatars saying how devastated they each were, how hard they prayed, how they wished they could stop the wind and stop the people (*who the hell did* this *anyway? who caused* this *to happen?*) from instigating these preventable devastations, how they weren't sure why the fires happened year after year after year.

I did not leave my own comment.

My belly was growing by incredibly small amounts – sesame seed, blueberry, kidney bean – it grew.

I didn't know yet the schedule, but I, we, were on one. All I knew was I was growing and the baby was growing, too.

If you don't listen carefully you may as well be using a Magic 8 Ball. And so, I started to feel more.

I had a treasure, and nobody knew except me. You were a treasure. A treasure inside, not a critic.

If it's in me.
It might be me.
It might, though it might not.
It's more like half me.
An extension of me and another.

The morning the wind stopped bringing smoke to our doorsteps, people took off their face masks. These masks are said to do nothing to protect the lungs from poor air quality but still, we wore them because a thin barrier felt better than having nothing – but it really was nothing, nothing but a poor attempt at filtering what toxins we could – so we placed them over our noses and mouths every morning until it no longer made sense.

This act was about control.

Our summers are getting hotter. Next summer, will you be breathing the wildfire smoke with me? The dirty drift I can't protect you or your lungs from when your breath is your own?

That summer I took as much air as I needed for both of us and tried to let it all out, fully, to drain my body of all that I inhaled. The heavy air around me fueled me because that's all there was to feed my starving lungs, capillaries.

I was sick and dizzy and sucking back wildfire drift, and the smoke was getting more aggressive, penetrating rooms within rooms and both sides of the window glass.

We were told to stay indoors, but even inside was a container for smoke, a container in which we waited.

This is all true and happened when I was a vessel for you.

on the bus through Surrey to work,

"Fuck you, cunt"

when I move with my growing treasure past the man blocking the rear exit, his 8 a.m. Metallica through a Bluetooth speaker.

From a yet-to-be mother: seven months pregnant. Twenty-eight weeks, three days.

Commenters note a popping belly.

Dehydration. No swelling in fingers and toes. Insomnia. Attempts to sleep early die in the middle of the night. Night is reserved for tossing and turning.

How come my brain doesn't work like it used to? Hormones, I think, or a stranger at the helm. A mind that can't work how it used to work. Bursts of energy fade, soon.

What's the matter with you?

I was unsure. Search for a porthole into the belly. I couldn't be sure. Lack of focus. A container. Looking glass. Warm belly pop. Gathering. I don't know how all this will impact the baby. A container has certain requirements. Care is one of them.

Kicks to the belly. Brain power.

SEVERE.

SEVER.

SERVER.

An exclusive call to this time.

What do I think of this transition so far?

Well, I don't know what makes a good story, so I draw a vertical line on a page.

At this point, when I make a mistake or forget to do something with intention and awareness, it's said I have baby brain.

This is the idea that my pregnant brain has become so overwhelmed with extra blood and hormones that even simple tasks like remembering to send an email on time or checking in on a particular project is lost in a sea of hormones, never to surface again.

Forgetting to remember is a loss, a loss that is quickly attributed to carrying another human. A girl.

I'm thirty-six weeks pregnant. Set to be a first-time mom in less than one month. Always comments about my body, *how is your mood today?*

I've always been better at beginnings than at endings. The end of pregnancy, the beginning of parenthood.

This room I'm in is nestled in a house, which sits on a street, in behind Highway 1. The sun, cloaked in smoke, blazes red like Mars in the middle of the day and falls hard, flat. I've been confused and worried. We should stay inside.

It's okay to miss the blue sky.

Online, I watch an animated graphic explaining in technical detail how wind propels wildfire forward, how it jumps from one roof to another, and why this makes it so hard to manage the fire.

Online, I read a story about a man who attempts to save his home from the jumping flames with his garden hose.

This is how we work together: a baby in the belly.

A brain with a baby in the belly and a kick from the inside.

A belly tuned a bell. A tough look at tough tough love.

I wish I were a landslide.

I wish I were an electronic synthesizer.

I wish I could figure out how to stay in my lane without gazing in on others around me.

The paint we used to trim our baby's room was so old it'd become a jar of lunar crater crumbles. Limbs in the belly. An elbow stuck out above my belly button. She's not ready to enter this world, which is good.

A relief.

We're not ready either. It's a long way down. It's a long time coming. She won't remember how she shook my belly from the inside out with her moves, but I will.

A wandering path
from yet-to-be
to mother.

From mother
to mothering.

What is mothering?

TALENT

2 a.m.
Someone bangs
huge barrels
of cooking grease
in the pub parking lot
next to our
house.

Oh the rhythm!

Our neighbour thinks
the drummer is
a natural.
Eventually we all forget
the tune
sing the last
commercial
we heard instead.

I've listened
to the moment's
favourite song
so many times
at this point.
I worry when it's not
stuck in my head.

THIEVES AT WORK

Hope washed that inside-out heart
of mine with dirt. Shook it
water balloon, squeezed it jelly.
Rang it clean
again in the company of 1,763
intimate friends.

They've come to lull me. Pat
my burnt hair unique
qualify my ripped nylons kitsch.
If only they got my address wrong
once. I'd store my thoughts
away in air-tight Mason jars
watch them swim around, float
belly up.

REPEAT (III)

I went shopping to try new glasses over my old ones then lunched just outside the government office. On the balcony I found certainty underneath a stone. She jumped toward me and I saw every organ and bone in her body shimmer. It was then my blood multiplied without help. She tucked herself back into the fire and I let the heat burn my skin redder, thicker. Finally I became tangible, something to hang a hook on to admire. Scarlet. After a lunch of squid and carrot sticks, when I looked at my feet, my shoes all but blended into the tile. I pulled them out. In lieu of two footprints, I left a mound of rubble. Footless, I skipped home over a pool of calm soy milk. Two skips, then sink. If I had a pocket of pennies, I'd leave forgotten cents under escalator tracks to make my mark.

JUMPING JACKS

Blood and bone.
Caution and quality.
Go up the stairs and sign the papers.
Extra help and leisure time.
Most people aren't the least bit bad.
Gray hair and running shoes.
Order and pay.
Fear and bonus stars.
Cold shoulder and secret organic garden.
Aligned and maligned.
Most people think they can lead.
Play away and cry out.
Pick up and slam down.
Weepy eye and LED screen.
Most people can give you a reason.
Reasons why and reasons not.
Exercise and work.
Middle manager and icy banana.
Pay day and milkmaid.
Resources and human resources.
Humans and sources.
Ands and ampersands.
& & &.

WAKING UP

The good in my chest fidgets

Push, and find a high-functioning team canned and forlorn

In the mornings, I put on my uniform

It was practically night when I tied the apron around my waist

Age is nothing but a number until we go to the bank

Take a minute

Welcome each other to each other

This will be the neighbourhood bonding exercise

Take this poem as an encouraging nudge to find room in notches
and keyholes

In a moment when flavour is code for bitter

How do we use language?

Take a minute

The city searches for its coffee-club card

The mother brought the daughter to Starbucks to hear the Primerica
lady speak

I don't remember the cause

Swing this labour up for me as collaboration

This environment is so supportive

I'm always startled we aren't there yet

LANDSCAPING

This block
keeps us

I can't
place where

this house
and

that street
and

a picture
tells stories

of front yards
how our

walk
ages

in half
shadow

BLOOD

Tether dual vibrations
I say, *here we are*

Self-reflection is self-
sided, scaling

living room's memory
I won't find sea

change or
loyal practice.

I know I was cold here skin
raw from the super

good for me
I wait

for variable weather
a moment to slip through to you

to turn over
the pass-over plan

until I know it so well
I can do no better.

GO FIGURE

We'd both heard Dire Straits' "Money for Nothing" four times in a single week.

Couldn't believe it.

It's the world we live in.

My other brain song goes do, do, do, do, do, do.

Nothing to worry about.

Repetition is meant to pick us up and pull us flat.

Efficiency is meant to catapult us across the fence without pain.

Insurance is meant to keep us whole in light of the unexpected.

When we find out we hold the wrong insurance, we're politely urged to try again.

We try because we should desire to try, and extend our arms with the most visible veins forward.

We let the bank nurse take our blood.

We watch her file it, then wait and listen to the radio.

Let's go, go, go, go, go, go.

Away, away, away, away, away.

Forward momentum only.

REPEAT (IV)

There is a faded building
in the centre of town
that was a clearance store
for a major chain.

Special deals.

A spot to get a new patio set
in the middle of December, a
Christmas tree in May.

All cheap. Best prices.

The closing-out sales lasted years
until it was done for good.

I'll call to tell the rust I'm growing you is beautiful,
and blooming on the busted spokes
of the shopping cart I untangled
from the blackberry bush overtaking the ditch.

ACKNOWLEDGMENTS

Early versions of poems from this book have appeared in the following magazines: CV2, *Golden Handcuffs Review*, EVENT, *echolocation, Poetry Is Dead, touch the donkey, dusie*, and *The Capilano Review*. Thank you to their editors.

Thank you to Jordan Strom, curator at the Surrey Art Gallery, for including my *Surrey City Centre Née Whalley* sound and text installation in the January–February 2015 program, which included excerpts from "Moon Schedule" and "In the Afternoon."

Thank you, Cecily Nicholson, Catriona Strang, and the team at Talonbooks who helped shape and bring this manuscript to life.

Gratitude to my family, Tammy, Brandon, Joanne, and Brian for the stories, the love and support over the years. I sure needed it. To Gord, many of these poems are in your memory. To Aaron for the constant inspiration and encouragement.

And to my darling Esther, thank you for choosing me.

Taryn Hubbard's poetry, fiction, reviews, and interviews have been included in journals such as *Canadian Literature / Littérature canadienne, Room, The Capilano Review, Canadian Woman Studies,* CV2, *filling Station,* and others. She holds a B.A. in English and Communications from Simon Fraser University, and a certificate in journalism from Langara College. She lives in Chilliwack, BC, with her family. *Desire Path* is her first book.